Advanced Academic English

A handbook for university writing with glossary

Dina Awad

Grosvenor House
Publishing Limited

This book is published by
Grosvenor House Publishing Ltd
Link House
140 The Broadway, Tolworth, Surrey, KT6 7HT.
www.grosvenorhousepublishing.co.uk

A CIP record for this book
is available from the British Library

ISBN 978-1-80381-479-7
eBook ISBN 978-1-80381-480-3

Contents

Introduction   vii

Writing skills   xi

1. Steps   1

    1.1 Choosing a research topic   1

         Defining the context   2

         Controversy   3

         A good research topic   4

         Sections   5

    1.2 Sources   6

         Reliability   7

         Online Search   10

    1.3 Analyse   11

    1.4 Organise   12

         Information   12

         Layout   13

	1.5	Format	16
		Punctuation	17
	1.6	Citing	18
		Direct quotes	20
		Secondary citations	21
2.	Parts		22
	2.1	Introduction	22
	2.2	Paragraphs	23
	2.3	Conclusion	26
3.	Connect		27
	3.1	Order	27
	3.2	Cross reference	28
		Similarity	32
		Difference	33
	3.3	Logical flow	34
4.	Opinion		35
	4.1	I agree	35
	4.2	I disagree	36

5.		Academic Language	37
	5.1	Outline	38
	5.2	Paragraph starters	39
	5.3	Reference verbs	40
		Examples of reference verbs	41
	5.4	Caution	42
	5.5	Time	46
	5.6	Dictionary use	48
6.		Structure	49
	6.1	State	49
	6.2	Explain	50
	6.3	Support	51
	6.4	Compare	52
		Similarities	53
		Differences	54
	6.5	Analyse	55
	6.6	Criticise	56
		Academic sources	56
		Media sources	57

	International Organisations	58
	Governmental reports	59
6.7	Vary structure	61
7.	Avoid!	62
	Large goals	62
	Personal pronouns	64
	Generalisations	65
	Emphasis	67
	Emotional	68
	Idioms	69
	Proverbs	70
	Functional keywords in search	72
	Format	73
	Style	74
	Discrimination	75
	Plagiarism	76
8.	Glossary	77

Introduction

This book is a compilation of teaching materials developed over many years of teaching in higher education institutions in both the UK and abroad at both graduate and postgraduate levels. The carefully selected collection of original materials were presented in lectures to help students improve their writing style, diction and content organisation.

This academic writing handbook offers explicit and concise guidelines in the form of short sample phrases that can be used directly without lengthy and complicated instructions. The simple points format is set to facilitate learning by making the layout more modern and user-friendly so that the digital-age learner would not be discouraged by small dense text. Therefore, a presentation similar to that of short messages on social media would look more attractive and less studious. Although some websites and social media pages do have helpful advice and could hypothetically serve the same purpose, most of such content remains largely unsolicited and sporadic. On the other hand, information available in academic and professional websites is usually heavily laden with specialised jargon and descriptive terminology.

Unlike many textbooks and websites that instruct students on what should be used, this glossary acts as a post-writing editor that assists students in checking their drafts after being written, to meet higher-education quality. This all-inclusive academic handbook caters for all disciplines, especially those that require writing argument essays, reports and term papers in addition to dissertations and theses. Academic writing skill is no longer solely exclusive to humanities fields. Rather, it has now become a crucial requirement across disciplines such as Business Studies and Sciences. The information presented in this book can also help practitioners in higher education across disciplines. The quick ready-made phrasal options can be projected as slides in revision sessions. Students, authors and researchers can use the handbook as a reference if they are not certain about certain expressions or formats. Professional proofreaders would benefit from the advice in an editing capacity. Therefore, the guidance, the usage-based phrases and the glossary assists native speakers of English whose automated writing expressions stem more from their casual spoken register. This group has been long neglected in English language education.

The glossary part at the end lists academic alternatives to some of the most common expressions of informal English produced by native and non-native speakers alike. The informal, less academic choices in the glossary were all collected from students' papers over years of teaching academic English at university level. Since academic English is no one's first language, it is time to identify its unspoken rules and traditions and present them simply and succinctly.

Writing skills

- A completed draft is better than a perfect paragraph
- Cite all sources in your text
- Use reference verbs
- Use plurals to generalise:
  - Researchers have found that
  - In most cases
  - Studies have shown that
- Full term on first mention of acronym:
  - English for specific purposes (ESP)
  - Teaching English to speakers of other languages (TESOL)

1. Steps

1.1 Choosing a research topic

- Is it important?
- Is it recent?
- Is it controversial?
- Is it popular?
- Are you interested in it?

Defining the context

Select time, place and group affected:

- Time (*lately, in the last five years, since 2020*)
- Country, city, region
- Type
- Ethnicity
- Profession, Industry
- Age group
- Gender

Controversy

- There are many views about the causes of this problem
- There are many views about the effects of this problem
- There is more than one solution to this problem
- Some think it is not a problem

A good research topic

- Recent, current (last five years)
- Important, crucial, essential, significant, relevant
- Popular, discussed in the media
- Controversial, debatable

Sections

In non-original research (you synthesise information from publications):

- Introduction
- Body paragraphs by topic (*causes, effects, solutions, ...* etc.)
- Conclusion

In original research

This is only when *you* collect the data:

- Introduction
- Literature review
- Method
- Results
- Discussion
- Conclusion

1.2 Sources

The most reliable information can be found in peer-reviewed academic journals.

You can find journal articles in:

- Your university library
- Google Scholar
- Academic databases

Other academic sources can be found in working papers published by universities:

- websites in ac (Britian, New Zealand, Canada)
- Websites ending in edu (American universities)

Reliability

Highly reliable

- University websites
  - .ac.
  - .edu
- University libraries
- University electronic libraries
- Google Scholar

Reliable: Non-academic

- Professional magazines (e.g. *National Geographic*)
- Non-profit organisations (.org)
- Government reports (.gov)
- Peer-reviewed professional books

Least reliable

Companies (.co, .com)
Books that are not peer-reviewed books
Personal blogs
Magazines
Tabloids

Online Search

- Use reliable search engines
- Use seven to ten key words
- Replace keywords with synonyms
- Select publications that are more recent
- Opt for the frequently cited.

1.3 Analyse

Add **depth** to each point you make, rather than list information:

- Give reasons
- Compare different views
- Describe reliability of sources
- Criticise sources (views, genre of publication, research method)
- Add possible causes and reasons
- Compare views about causes
- Describe results (high, low, sufficient)
- Compare results (higher, lower, more confident, less efficient)
- Add exceptions
- Add expectations and suggestions
- Compare solutions and suggestions

1.4 Organise Information

- Define
- Describe context (time and place)
- Background
- Outline main points
- Causes before effects
- Evidence from sources after each main point
- Direct causes before indirect causes
- Short-term effects before long-term effects
- Norms before exceptions
- Suggestions/possible solutions

Layout

Essay *vs.* Research paper

Essay

- Introduction paragraph
- Argument with examples
- Opposite argument with examples
- Conclusion

Research paper

- Introduction paragraph
- Argument with examples from published sources + opposing view
- Argument with examples from published sources + opposing view
- Argument with examples from published sources + opposing view
- Conclusion

Essay

- Introduction (10–20%)
- Body (75–90%)
- Conclusion (5–10%)

Research Paper

- Introduction
- Section headings
  - Types
  - Difficulties
  - Causes
    - Direct
    - Indirect
  - Effects
    - Short term
    - Long term
  - Possible solutions
- Conclusion
- References

1.5 Format

- Use recommended margins
- Write in paragraphs
- Double space (except the end references list)
- Font: Times New Roman 12 or Calibri 11
- Indent paragraphs
- Do not indent after headings and subheadings

Punctuation

- Full stop **after** reference bracket if at the end
- Space after comas and full-stops, not before.
- Do **not** use brackets if the author's name is part of the sentence
- Write numbers from one to ten as words
- Write numbers over ten as numerals

1.6 Citing

All information **must** be referenced.

Follow the reference system of your department[1]

- Refer to academic sources by author(s) surname
- If two authors, use both surnames
- If more than two authors, use first author surname followed by **et al**.
- Do not include the journalist's name or surname.
- Refer to a previously mentioned source as **ibid** if in the same paragraph
- Refer to information from media sources by name of newspaper or website
- Refer to information from organsiations by name of organisation.

---

[1] Such as Harvard, APA, MLA, Chicago, etc.

Academic journals and peer-reviewed books

- Refer to the research by author(s) surname and year
- Do not mention journal name, month or volume number in in-text citations
- If more than two authors, use first author's surname followed by et al.

Direct quotes

- Avoid direct quotes
- If important, keep direct quotes few and far between
- Keep quotes very short
- If long, indent as paragraph
- Reference quote with author, year and page number

Secondary citations

Use the source you do not have, then cite the source you found it in:

- According to Smith (2018, cited in Jacobs, 2020, p. 234)
- Include Jacobs 2020 only in your final list of references

2. Parts

2.1 Introduction

Maximum 20%

- Thesis statement: one sentence as main idea of the research
- Context: time and place
- Importance of the topic: explain its effect
- Short background: past events that led to this issue
- Outline: main parts of the paper
- No tables, pictures, charts or diagrams
- Avoid citations or references

2.2 Paragraphs

<u>One</u> controlling idea per paragraph.

Examples of paragraph topics:

- Direct causes
- Indirect causes
- Short term effects
- Long term effects
- Difficulties or challenges
- Possible solutions

Each paragraph **must** include:

- Topic sentence (short—main idea summary of the paragraph)
- Examples with evidence (in-text citations)
- Different information from different sources
- Comparison of views
- Evaluation and criticism

Each paragraph **could** include:

- Further explanation
- More details with evidence
- Similar views from publications
- Opposing views of authors and publications
- Facts, statistics, figures
- Personal opinion
- Conclusive sentence (thus, therefore, hence)

Sample topic sentences

- Most researchers agree that
- There are several types of
- There could be a number of causes for this issue.
- The... might have considerable effects on
- There are numerous solutions to this problem
- This issue can have long-term effects

2.3 Conclusion

The shortest paragraph of your paper (Maximum 10%):

- Connector (Finally, in conclusion, in short)
- Main idea (paraphrased from introduction)
- Very short summary (optional)
- Future expectations
- Recommendations for further research

3   Connect

3.1 Order

- The first/The second
- One of the
- The other
- The following
- Firstly/Secondly/Thirdly
- Finally
- In conclusion

3.2 Cross reference

- The previous
- The former
- (See Section 1)
- (See Chapter 2)
- The latter
- Next
- The following chapter will discuss this in more detail.

Forward reference

- This will be discussed further in the following section
- Further details will be discussed
- The next section/chapter
- This paper will review

Back reference

- As explained in the previous section
- See Chapter 1/Chapter 2
- As mentioned above
- The latter

Ending

- This section has demonstrated that
- This chapter has reviewed
- This paper has considered

Similarity

- Similarly
- Both
- Along the same lines
- Jacobs (2020) agrees with Smith (2018)
- Jacobs (2020) concedes with Smith's (2018) views in the sense that
- Jacobs (2020) extends Smith's (2018) proposal that
- Jacobs (2020) supports Smith's proposal to

Difference

- In contrast
- However
- On the other hand
- Conversely
- Unlike
- Another view
- Alternatively

3.3 Logical flow

- Rather
- Thus
- Hence
- Since
- Therefore
- Despite
- Consequently
- Although
- Instead
- Because

4. Opinion

4.1 I agree

In research, you show that you agree with an opinion without using 'I':

- There is a strong belief that
- Researchers agree that
- It is evident that
- It is clear that
- It could be argued that
- It is true that
- A compelling view is that
- It is noticeable that
- It has been shown that
- Research proves that
- Many researchers believe that

4.2 I disagree

- Author (year) did not offer a comprehensive explanation about
- Author et al. (year) claim that
- It is unclear whether
- The solution offered by Author (year) is hardly practical
- There is some inaccuracy in Author's (year) view
- The research failed to address some major concerns regarding
- Some researchers argue that
- It is not clear whether
- Some argued that... yet
- It is questionable/doubtful that
- This argument can be faulty because
- This argument might not be effective, since
- It is hard to apply in other contexts
- The study failed to include

5. Academic Language

5.1 Outline

This study/paper will:

- show
- present
- review
- examine
- describe
- find out whether there is
- explore
- suggest
- offer
- revisit
- re-address

5.2 Paragraph starters

Topic sentences are general and show the main idea of the paragraph:

- There are many possible reasons for
- There are several long term consequences for
- Most researchers agree that
- The main cause for this issue is
- Another possible effect could be
- Many experts believe that
- Starting a new business can be challenging
- Some studies show the benefits of
- Media sources hold a different view

5.3 Reference verbs

Report information from your academic sources using the author(s) name(s) (year) followed by:

- Believes
- Claims
- Suggests
- Argues
- Contends
- Holds
- States
- Advocates
- Discusses
- Finds
- Concludes
- Examines
- Considers
- Questions
- Maintains

Examples of reference verbs

The researchers hold that
Author (year) thinks that
The researcher believes that
This article reports a study on
Both Author (year) and Author (year) found that
This paper discusses the effects of
The results indicate that
The study concludes with
The research recommends
The paper suggests

5.4 Caution

Academic language is doubtful, careful and varies in degrees of certainty:

- Can
- Could
- Possibly
- Probably
- May
- Might
- Perhaps
- Would
- Likely

Cautious language can be used for

- Views
- Causes
- Explanations
- Effects
- Results
- Solutions
- Expectations

Cautious language can be hypothetical

- If
- Should
- In this case
- When

Examples of cautious hypothesis

- If this continues, it might lead to serious consequences
- This could mean increased costs for manufacturers
- One of the direct causes is possibly unemployment
- In this case, nurses would have to find another option
- There could be more than one interpretation
- It is expected that there would be an increase
- There would probably be a new system

5.5 Time

Views and opinions are always in the present

Even if the study is dated or the author had passed away:

- Believes
- States
- Holds
- Stresses
- Proposes
- Suggests

Events, methods, experiments and findings are always in the past

- Used
- Analysed
- Discovered
- Found that
- Created a formula
- Deduced that
- Compared

5.6 Dictionary use

- Use a dictionary from your first language **to** English
- Finish reading the paragraph before using a dictionary
- Try to guess the meaning from the context
- Use a dictionary more in **writing** tasks
- Use a dictionary more for **synonyms** than meaning
- Always read a full sentence example before you use a new word!

6. Structure

6.1 State

- State your opinion
- State an observation
- State a common view
- State a fact

6.2 Explain

- Paraphrase
- Exemplify
- Give reasons:
  Actual (cite)
  Your opinion (use hedging)
  Indirect causes
- Expect outcomes, effects and results:
  Present: short-term effects
  Future: long-term effects

6.3 Support

For each opinion, observation and statement you write, make sure it is supported by at least one of the following:

- **Reasons**: logical deduction, causes, rationale
- **Examples**: real event that actually happened (time and place)
- **Statistics**: from academic, professional, government and organisational sources
- **Evidence**: findings from research and publications

6.4 Compare

Comparing sources is part of all academic writing.

Compare your sources

- Opinions and views
- Reliability
- Objectivity
- Causes
- Responsibilities
- Effects
- Methods of research
- Expectations and projections
- Solutions

Similarities

- Similarly
- Both authors agree that
- Smith (2018) agrees with Victor (2016) about the need for renewable energy
- Along the same lines, the Guardian newspaper (2021) states that
- Smith (2018) extends Victor's (2016) view that
- Recent studies (Jacobs 2020) confirm former propositions that there is a need for change

Differences

All types of research papers should point out differences between publications, especially in literature reviews.

Sentence initial

- On the other hand
- However
- In contrast
- Conversely
- Alternatively

Mid-sentence

- While
- Whereas
- But

6.5 Analyse

Add depth to your writing by presenting _possible_ reasons
and consequences:

- This could probably be caused by
- Which might lead to
- May be interpreted as
- Possibly implying that
- Long term effects can include
- This could cause… in the short term
- There is a chance that
- One of the indirect causes could be
- Which may result in
- There is a likelihood

6.6 Criticise

Critical thinking is expected in all research papers.

Mention gaps, limitations and shortcomings of your sources.

Academic sources

- This article has a number of limitations, such as
- A key weakness in this study is
- There is a lack of
- The concept might not apply to other contexts
- The sample is biased, since
- The method did not include
- The author failed to address
- The findings might be outdated

Media sources

If some of your sources are not academic, you can question the motivation and the purpose:

- Propaganda
- Bias
- Political motives (right wing/left wing)
- Lacks evidence
- Anecdotal evidence
- Does not depend on reliable sources
- Reflects the journalist's personal view
- There is some doubt regarding the credibility of this paper

International Organisations

Reports from international organisations such as the UN are largely reliable and trustworthy, but if:

- Might be outdated
- Have insufficient information
- Does not cover certain regions, groups
- Misleading

Governmental reports

- These websites are useful if they have survey results or population data.
- They can be reliable or not depending on the country and its policy.
- Democratic countries usually have reliable data.
- Search for evidence that proves whether the information is propaganda or reflects actual statistics.

Examples of critical expressions

- The author does not address
- Little details are given
- The researcher(s) did not consider
- This publication makes no attempt to
- This study fails to mention
- The number of participants is insufficient
- There is no specific evidence regarding
- The results cannot be applied to different contexts
- The paper does not account for
- The authors did not include
- There needs to be further evidence regarding
- There are few facts that prove

6.7 Vary structure

Repetition is a sign of weakness.

Change the way you start sentences:
- Start with a preposition (by, in, on, at, for)
- Start with an adverb (firstly/most importantly/ finally)
- Start with a demonstrative (This, these, that, those)
- Start with a connector (other, another)
- Start with an ordinal (the first/the second/the third)
- Start with numbering or quantifier (one of the, some, most, few)
- Start with the subject (author's name, the researchers)
- Start with a comparative (However, Similarly, On the other hand, in contrast)
- Start with example: (For example, for instance, one case in point)

7. Avoid!

Large goals

Do not promise to:

- prove
- solve a problem
- cover an entire topic
- find a solution for a problem
- discover
- reveal

Instead, use terms such as: this paper will:

- Review

- Address

- Compare

- Discuss

- Analyse

- Consider

Personal pronouns

Academic writing is impersonal. Therefore, avoid referring to yourself and other individuals.

- I
- We
- You
- Our
- Us
- My
- Your

Generalisations

Academic writing is specific. Avoid sweeping statements and absolute views and judgements.

- All
- Every
- Each
- Ever
- Never
- Always
- Whole
- Entire
- Totally

Exaggerations

Try to avoid absolutes and exaggerations such as:

- Greatest
- Best
- Worst
- Disaster
- Tragedy
- Terribly

Emphasis

- Very
- Really
- Too
- So
- Very
- Truly
- Absolutely
- Definitely
- Extremely

Emotional

Academic writing is logical and, impersonal and unemotional. Avoid expressions such as:

- Sad
- Happy
- Distressed
- Thrilled
- Ecstatic
- Overjoyed
- Awful
- Miserable
- Depressing
- Annoying
- Exciting

Idioms

Avoid academic writing is factual and logical. Avoid idiomatic and figurative expressions.

- At the end of the day
- Flying colours
- A leap of faith
- Sit on the fence
- The ball is in their court
- Shining success
- Sea of grief
- As cold as ice

Proverbs

Academic writing is realistic and practical. Do not use proverbs or famous sayings.

- The grass is greener on the other side
- Honesty is the best policy
- Actions speak louder than words
- You reap what you sow
- Hope for the best
- Practice makes perfect

Short forms

Academic writing is formal. Contractions are a sign of informal communication and should be avoided.

- Isn't
- Aren't
- Didn't
- Won't
- We've
- It's
- They'll

Functional keywords in search

When searching for information online, do not use the following:

- In, on, at, over, above, below, next, through, by
- No, not, none, never, un
- A, an, the
- Can, could, may, might, will, would
- What, who, where, when
- Is, are, was, were, be

Format

- Do not indent after section headings
- Do not write in BLOCK CAPITALS
- Do not use diagrams or charts unless you collected the data
- Do not use pictures
- Do not underline text
- Do not use frames
- Do not use coloured text
- Do not use (parentheses) to explain
- Do not use question form?
- Do not use more than one full-stop. . .
- Do not change font type or size in the body of the text
- Do not use exclamation marks!
- Do not use **bold** font in body paragraphs

Style

There are some unwritten rules of good academic style.

It is best to avoid

- Repetition—use synonyms
- 'and' more than once in each sentence
- Using 'which', 'where', 'who' or 'that' more than once in one sentence
- Many quotes or long quotes
- Rhetorical and open ended questions
- Starting with And, But, Also, So
- Short form: phone, intro, ASAP, photos, info, gov.
- Double negatives in one sentence
- Authors' first name or initials

Discrimination

Academic writing is politically correct. Be extra careful by avoiding all expressions that distinguish one group as better or less than the others.

These include:

- race
- gender (chairman, mankind, postman)
- nationality
- body size/shape
- sexual orientation
- age
- physical or mental disability

Plagiarism

- Avoid copying information
- Reference all information by citing its source
- Mention the author(s), year of publication and page number
- Paraphrase text
- Use synonyms
- Restructure (switch the sentence: forward, backward)
- Change voice (active/passive)
- Use AI applications to edit your text
- Do not use AI to create content

8. Glossary

This part of the book will offer you formal alternatives to informal, spoken English.

Less Academic	More Academic
A couple of	Several
	Few
A lot of	Multiple
	Multitude
	Plenty
	Abundance
	Numerous
A while	Some time
Abnormal	Less frequent
	Exceptional
Above board	Legal
	Acceptable
Absolutely	Surely

Less Academic	More Academic
Act out	Enact
	Perform
	Deploy
	Respond
	Express
Add up	Reasonable
	Logical
	Sensible
Add up to	Result in
All	Most
	Many
	In general
	In most cases
	The majority of
Already	As discussed in Chapter
Always	Frequently
	Predominantly
	Regularly
	Usually
Amazing	Impressive
	Commendable
	Effective
And so on	Among others

Less Academic	More Academic
Anything	Item
	Factor
	Most other
As (I) mentioned earlier	As mentioned earlier
As far back as	Since
Awesome	Effective
	Successful
	Significant
	Considerable
	Unexpected
Awesome	Positive
Back off	Retreat
	Recoil
	Recede
Back off	Retreat
	Withdraw
Back then	In the past
	At the time
Back up	Support
	Evidence
	Proof
Backing	Support
	Evidence

Less Academic	More Academic
Bad	Negative
	Disadvantageous
	Drawback
	Shortcoming
	Weakness
	Limitation
Bail out	Withdraw
Bank on	Depend on
	Rely on
Barge in	Interrupt
	Intercept
Besides	In addition to
Best	More useful
	Better
	More effective
Big deal	Serious
	Sizeable
	Significant
Bit by bit	Gradually
Block	Prevent
	Exclude
Blow away	Positive effect
Blurt out	State
	Mention

Less Academic	More Academic
Boil down to	Can be summarised as
	In short
	Simply
Book	Reserve
Boss	Leader
	Manager
Bother	Irritate
Break	Interrupt
Break down	Divide
	Classify
	Categorise
	Pause
	Halt
	Cease
	Fail
Break out	Spread
	Start
	Increase
	Unfold
Breakthrough	Success
	Succeed
Bring about	Cause
	Lead to

Less Academic	More Academic
Bring around	Convince
	Reason
	Persuade
Bring out	Elicit
	Reveal
Bring up	Raise
Bring up (topic)	Mention
	Discuss
	Review
Bundle	Package
	Group
	Set
Burn out	Lose enthusiasm
	Exhaust
Burst	Erupt
	Rupture
Buy into	Believe
	Follow
	Agree with
	Become convinced about
Call for	Necessitate
Call off	Cancel
Calm down	Become quiet
	Settle

Less Academic	More Academic
Carry on	Continue
	Progress
	Develop
Carry out	Conduct
	Administer
	Perform
Carry through	Continue
Cast aside	Exclude
Catch up	Update
	Draw closer
Chase up	Follow
	Pursue
Check out	Investigate
	Examine
Clear away	Remove
Clear up	Clarify
Cling to	Keep
	Hold
Close in	Approach
Close on	Approximate
Close up	Close
Come across	Meet
	Encounter

Less Academic	More Academic
Come apart	Divide
	Separate
Come around to	Agree
Come back	Return
Come by	Meet
Come up with	Produce
	Create
	Discover
Cons	Shortcomings
	Disadvantages
Correct	True
	Accurate
Count against	Disprove
Cover up	Conceal
Cut (down)	Reduce
	Decrease
Cut off	Disconnected
	Disengaged
	Far
Cut out	Modelled
	Designed
Dangerous	Serious
Dead end	End
	Final stage

Less Academic	More Academic
Definitely	Indeed
Die away	Fade gradually
	Disappear
Die out	Fade
	Disappear
Disaster	Adversity
Do with	Benefit from
	Take advantage of
Do without	Forgo
Done	Finished
	Completed
Doubts (verb)	Questions
Down the line	Consequently
	Eventually
Downside	Shortcoming
	Weakness
	Flaw
	Drawback
Draw up	Plan
Drop	Dismiss
	Omit
	Overlook
	Disregard

Less Academic	More Academic
Dumb	Unreasonable
	Impractical
Each	Some
	Most
	The vast majority
Ease off	Ease
Eerie	Strange
	Exceptional
Entire	All
	Most
	The majority
Etc.	Among others
	X, Y and Z
Even	Including
	As well as
Even if	Including instances
	As well as cases
Even though	Despite
	Although
Ever	Unlikely
Ever more	Gradually
	Steadily
	Increasingly

Less Academic	More Academic
Every	Some
	Most
	The majority of
Evil	Negative
	Harmful
Excellent	Quality
	Successful
	Effective
Face up to	Challenge
Fall back	Contingency
	Emergency
Fall back on	Depend
	Utilise
	Substitute
Fall for	Become disillusioned with
	Believe
Fall out	Disagree
Fallout	Consequences
	Results
Fantastic	Successful
	Impressive
Feel down	Unhappy
	Unfortunate

Less Academic	More Academic
Feels like	Seems
	Appears to be
	Presents
Fend for	Provide
Figure	Understand
	Realise
Figure out	Understand
	Fathom
Fill in for	Replace
	Substitute
Find out	Explore
	Examine
	Consider
Finish with	Lay aside
	Disregard
	Conclude
First and foremost	Firstly
	Primarily
	Most significantly
	Most importantly
Fish for	Search
	Focus on
	Investigate

Less Academic	More Academic
Fix	Solve
	Repair
Fix up	Repair
	Solve
Flare-up	Outbreak
	Eruption
Flick	In a short time
	Quickly
	Abruptly
Folks	Individuals
	Members of the community
	Families
	Locals
Follow up	Pursue
	Continue
Fuming	Angry
	Negative
Gather up	Collect
	Sum
Get	Become
	Receive
	Acquire
	Obtain
	Have

Less Academic	More Academic
Get along	Survive
	Manage
	Cope
	Progress
Get around	Avoid
	Evade
Get away with	Evade
Get back	Return
Get by	Cope
	Manage
Get down	Descend
	Drop
	Decrease
	Fall
Get into	Immerse
Get off	Leave
	Depart from
	Disregard
Get out	Excuse
	Escape
	Avoid
Get over	Recover from
Get through	Pass

Less Academic	More Academic
Get through	Endure
	Persevere
Get through to	Convince
	Persuade
Give	Provide
	Offer
	Present
Give away	Provide freely
	Inform
	Unravel
Give in	Acquiesce
	Agree
Give in (to)	Acquiesce
	Agree
	Surrender
Give out	Distribute
Give up	End
	Forgo
	Cease
Give way to	Allow
	Permit
	Give access to

Less Academic	More Academic
Go after	Pursue
	Follow
	Seek
Go against	Disagree with
Go by	Rely
	Depend
Go down	Reduce
	Lessen
	Lower
Go for	Opt for
	Choose
	Select
Go in depth	Discuss in detail
	Deeply analyse
Go into	Discuss
	Elaborate
	Describe in detail
Go on	Pursue
	Continue
	Persist
Go through	Experience
	Enter
Go up	Increase

Less Academic	More Academic
Go up	Increase
	Rise
Go with	Combine
	Mix
Go wrong	Misjudge
	Deteriorate
	Become incorrect
	Err
	Make mistakes
Good	Positive
	Successful
	Efficient,
	Feasible
	Higher quality
	Better
Got to	Ought to
	Should
	Obliged to
Great	Successful
	Efficient
	Practical
	Valuable
	Positive

Less Academic	More Academic
Great deal	Plenty of
	Exceedingly
Gross	Unpleasant
	Uncultured
	Uncivilised
Grow into	Expand
	Realise
	Become
Grown-up	Adult
Guy	Man
	Young man
Hand in	Submit
Hang on	Persevere
	Continue
Happen	Occur
Have against	Disagree with
	Criticise
Hinges on	Depends on
	On condition
Hold against	Disagree with
Hold on	Persist
	Continue

Less Academic	More Academic
Hold out	Resist
	Withstand
	Persevere
Hold up	Delay
	Postpone
	Discontinue
Hold up	Last
	Persevere
	Endure
Hopeless	Smaller chance to succeed
Huge	Considerable
	Significant
Hugely	Greatly
	To a large extent
	Considerably
	Significantly
	Notably
In my opinion	It is evident that
	It seems that
	Clearly
	Evidently
	Notably
Incredibly	Excessively

Less Academic	More Academic
Iron out	Remove
	Dismiss
	Disregard
Job	Profession
	Occupation
	Task
	Duty
Just	Only
	Merely
	Solely
Keep back	Withhold
	Restrain
Keep from	Refrain
	Avoid
Keep on	Continue
Keep out	Leave
	Dismiss
	Omit
	Ban
	Bar
Keep up (with)	Continue
	Persevere
	Endure
	Withstand

Less Academic	More Academic
Kid	Child
Kind of	To a certain extent
	Fairly
	Rather
	Relatively
Last but not least	Finally
Lay down	Establish
Lay off	Make redundant
Lean on	Rely on
	Depend on
Leave out	Omit
	Dismiss
	Disregard
	Ignore
Let off	Forgive
	Permit
	Excuse
Let out	Publish
	Allow
	License
	Emit
Like	Such as

Less Academic	More Academic
Little to do with	Irrelevant to
	Dissociated from
	Disconnected
Loads	Many
	Numerous
	A large amount of
Look at	Consider
	Take into consideration
Look back	Reconsider
	Reassess
Look into	Examine
	Test
	Investigate
Look out (for)	Take into consideration
	Pay attention to
	Heed by
Look up	Search for
	Find
	Trace
	Examine
	Consider

Less Academic	More Academic
Lots of	Multiple
	Multitude
	Plenty
	Abundance
	Numerous
Mad	Angry
	Bizarre
Made up	Created
	Fabricated
Made up of	Consists of
	Comprises
Make	Produce
	Perform
	Generate
Make out	Discern
	Distinguish
	Deduce
	Discover
Make public	Announce
Make sure of	Ensure
	Guarantee
Make up for	Compensate

Less Academic	More Academic
Mark down	Reduce
	Devalue
	Demote
Marvellous	Successful
	Impressive
	Good quality
Mate	Friend
	Acquaintance
Maybe	Might
	Could
	Probably
Mess up	Err
	Commit an error
Mess up with	Violate
	Wrong (verb)
Mind	Object to
	Disagree
Miss out	Forgo
	Leave
	Exclude
Mix up	Confuse

Less Academic	More Academic
Move along	Agree with
	Develop
	Progress
Move on	Continue
	Change the subject
Move up	Ascend
	Progress
	Advance
Nail down	Understand fully
	Guarantee
	Succeed
Naturally	Known
	Expected
	Usual
	Commonly
Never mind	Regardless
	In addition to
	Notwithstanding
Nice	Pleasant
	Agreeable
Nice	Advantageous
	Acceptable
	Pleasant

Less Academic	More Academic
No-brainer	Simple
	Easy
Nobody	Few
	Almost no one
Normal	Average
	Known
Nothing	Little
	Few
Obviously	Clearly
	Expectedly
Of course	Usually
	As expected
On track	Progressing
	Continuing
	As expected
	To plan
Once again	Cf. Chapter...
Open up	Open
	Allow
	Permit
	Access
Out of shape	Extraordinary

Less Academic	More Academic
Outrage	Large effect on
	Strong effect on
	Increase
Pass for	Instead
	As
	Replace
Pass on	Communicate
	Transmit
	Deliver
Pass out	Distribute
Pass up	Forgo
People	The general public
	The population
	Individuals
	Users
	Consumers
Perfect	Useful
	Practical
	Applicable
	Successful
	Improved
	Advanced
	Efficient
	Logical
	Feasible

Less Academic	More Academic
Pick up	Collect
	Elicit
	Learn
Pick up (on)	Correct
	Criticise,
	React
	Respond
	Comment
Pile up	Accumulate
	Gather
	Compile
	Create a collection of
Point out	Focus
	Explain
Pretty	Very
	Consistently
	Considerably
	Significantly
	To a large extent
Prey on	Exploit
	Use
	Harm
	Mistreat
Pros	Advantages
	Benefits

Less Academic	More Academic
Pull down	Criticise
Pull off	Succeed
Put off	Delay
	Postpone
	Discourage
Put together	Devise
	Assemble
Put up (with)	Tolerate
	Endure
	Persevere
	Withstand
Really	Critically
	Crucially
	Effectively
	Significantly
Reckon	Believe
	Hold
	Think
Right	Accurate
	Correct
Right	Valid
	Feasible
	Accurate
	Possible
	Correct

Less Academic	More Academic
Right (politically)	More/less conservative
Roll back	Reduce
Same	Similar to
	Parallel with
	In accordance with
Says	Discusses
	Reviews
	Mentions
	Focuses on
	Presents
	Shows
	Demonstrates
	Suggests
	Reports
	Believes
See (something) through	Finish
	Complete
	Accomplish
	Achieve
	Fulfil
	Realise
See to	Address
Set about	Started
	Began

Less Academic	More Academic
Set up	Establish
	Create
Shocking	Surprising
	Unexpected
Sift through	Examine
	Search
	Explore
	Investigate
Size up	Assess
	Evaluate
Skip	Exclude
	Leave
	Drop
Slow down	Become less active
	Reduce
	Delay
	Weaken
So	Therefore
	Thus
	Hence
So	Very
	Extremely
	Greatly
So on and so forth	Among others

Less Academic	More Academic
Someone	An individual
	One
	A person
Somewhat	To a certain extent
	Can be considered
Sort	Kind
	Type
	Genus
Sort out	Organise
	Arrange
	List
	Itemise
	Resolve
	Rearrange
	Solve
Spectacular	Extraordinary
	Exceptional
Stand by	Support
Stand down	Leave
	Resign
Stand in for	Replace
	Substitute
	Represent

Less Academic	More Academic
Stand out	Distinguished
	Excel
Start off	Start
	Begin
	Embark on
Stay	Remain
	Keep
	Last
Stay away from	Avoid
Step back	Retreat
	Diminish
	Regress
Step in	Become involved
Still	Yet
	To this point
Stop by	Focus on
	Visit briefly
Straighten out	Resolve
Strange	Uncommon
	Irregular
	Infrequent
	Unexpected

Less Academic	More Academic
Strike out	Omit
	Delete
	Cancel
	Disregard
	Neglect
Stuck	Immovable
	Plateau
	Static
	Stable
	Remain in the same position
Stuff	Belongings
	Possessions
	Items
Stuffy	Old-fashioned
Stupid	Inaccurate
Such	To the extent that
	To a large degree
	A lot of
Take after	Resemble
	Follow
Take apart	Review in detail
	Assess separately
	Analyse
Take on	Accept

Less Academic	More Academic
Take over	Assume the position of
	Take control of
	Manage
Take time off	Discontinue
Takes (time)	Lasts
	Requires
Talk	Discuss
	Review
	Mention
	Focus on
	Present
Talks about	Discusses
	Reports
	Reviews
	Suggests
	Believes
Techie	Technical
	Technician
Tell	Relate
	Recount
The rest	The other
	The remaining

Less Academic	More Academic
Then	Hence
	Thus
	Consequently
	As a result
Thing	Factor
	Item
	Element
	Component
	Topic
	Notion
Though	Although
	Nonetheless
	However
Tie in	Agree with
	Link to
	Relevant to
	Associate with
Ties up with	Relates to
	Is relevant to
	Is similar to
Till	Until
Too	Largely
	Significantly
	Critically
	Crucially

Less Academic	More Academic
Too much	Excessive
	Unnecessary
Top up	Add to
	Increase
Touch on/upon	Mention
	Review
	Discuss briefly
Trade upon	Exploit
	Use
Try for	Attempt
Try out	Test
Turn down	Reject
Turn out	Produce
Ugly	Unpleasant
	Disagreeable
Up to	Until
	To the extent that
Up to (someone/something)	Depends largely on
	Relies on
	Subject to
Up to date	Recent
	Relevant

Less Academic	More Academic
Use up	Exhaust
	Expend
	Consume
	Deplete
Used to	Was
	Were
Very	Considerably
	Significantly
	To a large extent
Weird	Rare
	Unusual
	Different
	Exceptional
Went wrong	Misjudged
	Erred
	Mistook
	Deteriorated
Whenever	When
	At the time when
	In due course
	Once the occasion arises
Wherever	Possibly
	In many possible places
	In possible/likely locations

Less Academic	More Academic
Whoever/ whomever	Any Most people
Whole	All Most The majority
Wonderful	Positive Effective Advantageous Beneficial Fruitful Efficient
Worn out	Tired
Wrong	Inaccurate Misrepresented Faulty Less valid
You/your	One Individual

www.ingramcontent.com/pod-product-compliance
Lightning Source LLC
Chambersburg PA
CBHW051731040426
42447CB00008B/1081